Getting Along
with Your Friends

Getting Along with Your Friends

PHYLLIS REYNOLDS NAYLOR

Drawings by
Rick Cooley

Abingdon
Nashville

GETTING ALONG WITH YOUR FRIENDS

Library of Congress Cataloging in Publication Data

NAYLOR, PHYLLIS REYNOLDS.
 Getting along with your friends.
 SUMMARY: A self-help approach to making and getting
along with friends, exploring the purpose of friendship,
understanding the feelings and behavior of oneself and others,
and changing one's behavior.
  1. Childhood friendship—Juvenile literature. [1.
 Friendship. 2. Interpersonal relations]
I. Cooley, Rick. II. Title.
BF723.F68N39   158'.25   79-22999

ISBN 0-687-14122-2

To Vaughan
and all his buddies

CONTENTS

Getting Along
with Your Friends

WHAT'S A
FRIEND FOR?

For talking with. For walking with. A friend, like a family, is for sharing things together in a caring kind of way.

Unlike a family, however, we are not born into our circle of friends or adopted by them. We choose them and they choose us—sometimes for many, many years, sometimes for only a short while. Some people have many friends, others only a few. But it is how well we get along together that counts.

A real friend is more than just a person who sits beside you in class and laughs at your jokes. Friends are persons who are pleasant to know and nice to have around.

But a true friend is someone special. When Scouts go swimming, they use the buddy system. They pair off and each keeps an eye out for the other. Good friends are like buddies. They care about what happens to us and try to help when we need them. Good friends also bring out the best in us, not the worst, and are happy for our successes.

If good friends are that great, why do they argue sometimes—fight, even? Why do they get jealous or hurt each other? Why do they tease? Why can't friends always be loyal and considerate?

Because it's not a perfect world. The sun is not always warm, the wind not always gentle, and friends and families and nations do not always get along with each other, even though they would all be happier if they did.

But the nice thing about being a person and not a doorknob is that we can change. We can work to become thoughtful friends ourselves. And that's what this book is all about.

CHAPTER 1

THINGS COULD
ALWAYS BE BETTER

LOOKING AROUND

Friends can be found in the strangest places. The old woman who sits on her steps each afternoon may have some fascinating stories to tell—if somebody just took the time to stop and visit.

Hank Bailey's Dad has a great sense of humor. If you ever came by the garage some spring day when he's working on his boat, you might find it hard to stop laughing with him.

Laura's little sister is only six, but she makes the most creative things out of clay. Somebody could have a great time introducing Laura to pottery if he ever took her seriously.

The guard at the supermarket once ran in the

Boston marathon, and he's always looking for somebody to jog with on Sunday afternoons.

Claire Schiller, the girl with the artificial leg, has a record collection you wouldn't believe. She also has a set of Ludwig drums in her basement that she plays for special friends—if anyone makes an effort to get to know her.

Pete—the tall, shy kid in seventh grade—is building a pond in his backyard. He hopes to have it done by next April and is looking for somebody to help him raise frogs.

Everybody wants friends, though some people say they don't really need anyone—that they can get along okay by themselves. Other people feel they must have friends around all the time—that they can't possibly go for ice cream, see a movie, or do their homework all alone.

People who say that they don't really need anyone are really saying that they have been hurt somewhere along the way, and because of this hurt they are scared of trusting anybody's friendship.

People who want others around all the time are afraid of being alone—and are telling us that they don't have a very good opinion of themselves.

Fortunately, there is a happy in-between. There are people who like to be with others sometimes and also enjoy being by themselves. They know that problems do not seem so bad if you can talk them over with a friend, and good things seem twice as wonderful if you can share them with somebody else.

During periods when there isn't anybody else to share with, they don't feel as though it is the end of the world. They know it would be nice to have some friends around, but they can manage.

However, things could always be better. Just as no one's body is perfect, there is no such thing as a perfect friendship, either. We've all got a mole where it shouldn't be or a nose that's too big or a chin that's too small, and we can't do much about it. But we *can* do a lot toward getting along better with our friends.

What would you most like to change? Some people like the friends they've got, but wish they had more. Some wish they could change the way they get along together. And some wish

they could trade their friends for a new bunch.

Each of us is like other people in some ways and different in some ways. We can't decide what is best by comparing ourselves to someone else. We all come from different families and backgrounds. Some people make friends very easily; others are shy and find it more difficult to make friends. Some people may be satisfied with lots of friends, but no one really special. Others want several close friends whom they can confide in.

You can't go around collecting friends as though they were baseball cards. If someone else has nine good friends and you only have three, remember that numbers don't count unless you're running for election.

Do you enjoy your friends or do you use them? Do you see them as people to share things with or do you always think of how they might be useful to you?

Do you like Sylvia mostly because she has a lot of friends, and you think she will help you be more popular?

Do you hang around with Hugh because he gets good grades, and you might need his help?

Are you friends with Carl because his father

owns a hobby shop and you think he might give you a discount?

Take a good look at the friends you have right now. Decide whether you like them for themselves or for what they might be able to do for you. If you could make changes, where would you start?

People want to be liked for themselves, and that is the best place to begin.

TAKING STOCK

Make a list of your closest friends. Describe what they look like as well as their personality characteristics—something like this:

John Salinas

Short, dark-haired, sort of skinny but nice-looking; great sense of humor, but cuts up sometimes at school. Is really good on the drums. A fairly loyal friend, though he's too quick-tempered.

Leslie Baker

Medium height and weight, not too pretty. She's always nice when we're together, but sometimes she talks about me behind my back. She makes good grades in school, but doesn't have many friends.

Craig Kominsky

Looks like a football player and is good in almost every sport. Gets mostly B's in school. Everybody seems to like him. Sometimes we get along okay together and sometimes we don't. I guess I'm a little jealous of him, but he does tease a lot and I don't like that.

If you have been honest about your list, you will name both the good and bad points of each person on it.

The next step is to look for patterns. You may not see any at all, but rather a scrambled mixture of good looks and not-so-good looks, of silly and serious, of loud and quiet, of students who get A's and students who get C's . . . .

Or you may see that the list leans a little to one side—positively tilts, in fact! Strange, you may say to yourself, but every single person on it is sort of a goof-off in class. Or perhaps it is too much the other way. Almost everyone on your list is very serious.

Perhaps out of the five friends you mentioned, at least four are good-looking and popular. Possibly it is the opposite; most of the people on your list are not very attractive at all and have no friends other than those in their own small group.

It might be that all the names you mentioned are interested in the same thing—soccer or ten-speed bikes or stamp collecting.

Try to see how many patterns you can find and write them down.

THINKING IT OVER

The kind of friends we choose says a lot about what we think of ourselves.

Pam has never felt very pretty. She feels she is too fat, for one thing. Her grandmother always told her that her eyes didn't focus properly, and her brother kidded her about having big feet, and somehow, when she put everything together, Pam felt downright ugly.

The truth is, she isn't exactly pretty, but she never tries to be. She puts on the first clothes she can find in the morning because she always feels it's useless to fuss over herself. Most of the time she just jokes about it, as though she doesn't really care one way or another.

She does care. She cares enough about her feelings not to risk having them hurt more than necessary. And so she never tries to make friends with anyone she thinks would possibly turn her down. Instead, she chooses other girls who have some of the same problems she does—girls who are uncertain about how they look or how much they should weigh or whether they have any talents worth sharing.

They have become sort of a club, and they even have a secret language they use to make fun of the more popular kids in school. The more popular students, in turn, resent this little group that keeps off to itself and talks about them behind their backs, so they tease Pam and her friends.

The more Pam is teased the worse she feels, and the more she clings to the few friends who share her problems. It's a vicious circle that no one seems to know how to break.

Beverly has much the same problem. She really doesn't look so much different from the other girls in her class; she just *feels* different. Beverly has a beautiful older sister who seems to accomplish everything she ever tries to do, and compared to her, Beverly feels inferior.

The only way she can ever be likeable, she thinks, is to tag around after the most popular girls in school and do exactly what they do. If one of the girls comes to school in a certain type of jeans, Beverly begs and pleads with her mother to buy her the same kind. She wears the same jewelry the other girls wear and the same sneakers. She spends each day waiting to see what the other girls are going to do and where they are going to sit in the lunchroom. Then she watches to see which way they are going to walk home after school.

Just because Beverly chooses the most popular girls to hang around with does not mean that she herself is popular. Pam chooses the more unattractive girls as friends because she feels they will accept her; Beverly chooses the most popular girls because she hopes that will make everyone think she is popular too. But inside, it doesn't change a thing.

Ted has a lot of friends. Whenever there's a party, Ted is invited. The popular boys like him, the not-so-popular too, and girls feel comfortable around him. He will sit with anybody who is handy in the lunchroom, and never stops to see where the most popular group is sitting.

Teachers like him, and his grades are usually B's. Whenever anyone asks Ted to help out or to do a favor, he always says yes. People say you can count on Ted.

The problem is, and there *is* a problem, Ted says yes too much. He is fair to everyone except himself. He wants so much to be liked, popular, and dependable, and he is, that there is little energy left over for Ted himself. If he plans on going sledding after dinner but a friend asks him to come over and help him with math problems, Ted always helps with the math problems. If he wants the part of the one-legged pirate in the school play but finds out that someone else wants it too, Ted tries out for another part. If he is in a hurry to get home from school and play with his dog but a friend asks him to stop at his house and watch television, Ted watches television.

The result is that even though Ted is well liked and popular, he is not happy most of the time, but he isn't sure why.

Lenny and Ted seem very much alike. Lenny, too, is popular and invited to parties. He also gets along with his teachers and has as many not-so-popular people for friends as he has popular ones.

But Lenny has learned to be fair to himself. He has learned to say no politely, even if it makes someone angry.

When Doug wanted him to cancel his plans with another friend, for example, and spend the weekend at his house, Lenny told him courteously that he couldn't do it, that he would come over to Doug's house another time.

Doug was sullen for a few days, but he soon got over it. And though he never said so, he respected Lenny a little more. He realized that Lenny would never cancel plans with *him* just because he got a better offer somewhere else.

WHAT ABOUT YOU?

So much for Pam and Beverly and Ted and Lenny. It's you that's important. What kind of questions do you need to ask yourself? This will depend on the kinds of patterns you discovered in your own list of friends.

If most of your friends are members of the in-crowd, is there something that makes you wary of becoming friends with the more quiet or less attractive students? Do you feel that someone might identify you as one of the less popular persons? Do you think your reputation needs all the bolstering it can get?

Is there something in you that makes you feel a little more important when there's somebody else around who seems a little less important? Do you build yourself up when you have someone else to look down on?

If so, how do you really feel about yourself? Why do you need to do this?

Suppose, after looking over your list, you discover the opposite. Perhaps you are surprised to discover that none of the friends you mentioned are doing very well in school. Perhaps more than a few of them are troublemakers. Or maybe your list is just a fair-sized collection of people who, for one reason or another, are neither very popular nor attractive nor bright. If you think about it, you might even call them loners or losers.

If this is your list, do you feel the same way

about yourself? Are you afraid of the competition of being around more popular students? If you are the leader of the loners, does this give you a feeling of acceptance or importance that you are afraid you might not find somewhere else? Do you feel better being top person among the losers than low person on the totem pole among the more popular kids?

People who like themselves, who are confident of their own abilities, have many different kinds of friends. They may like Gary, who's quiet, because he's a good listener, and when he *does* speak up, it's usually something worth hearing.

They may like Janet because she's pretty and funny and good-natured. They may like Lois because she's a real brain and comes up with fantastic words for *Scrabble*.

Whenever they give a party, however, they invite John because, even though he's overweight and dresses sloppily, he's the best storyteller around. They may invite Sam, just because he's new, and Greg, just because he's lonely, and Dorothy, just to get to know her better. They aren't afraid to include people who don't have a lot of pluses—or to take a chance on somebody they hardly know at all.

Can we have friends who have values different from ours? It depends on how strong we are ourselves. If we can be swayed by a fast argument, or are not really sure of how we stand, perhaps not. People who feel confident about what they believe and how they behave don't feel threatened. They can be friends with many types of people, from many types of backgrounds.

If Terry is an interesting person at school but seems to get into trouble on weekends, by all means keep him as a friend at school as long as he respects you for what you are—and as long as you don't feel pressured to join him in doing things of which you don't approve.

Friendship starts on the inside. It means becoming a real pal, first of all, with yourself. If you met yourself for the very first time, would you like what you saw?

Maybe it's time to get acquainted.

CHAPTER 2

HOW TO BE YOURSELF WITHOUT HALF TRYING

WHO ELSE CAN YOU BE?

You can pretend you are Napoleon. You could wish you were someone on TV. But the fact remains that you are trapped inside your own skin and can never, even for an instant, be anybody else. You are the one and only, the original YOU.

If any of the other four hundred million spermatozoa racing to fertilize the ovum had got there first, you would have been somebody entirely different. It's miraculous really, when you think of the odds, that you were the one who succeeded. So before you read any further, wish yourself a happy birthday.

There are people who look something like

31

you. There are people who act like you. There are even people who have the same name. But not one of them *is* you. So you might just as well accept the wonderful fact that you are unique.

Some people spend their lives trying to be what they think other people want them to be. They never raise their voices around their grandmother because she doesn't like to see people upset. When they're around Bobby Sims all they talk about is sports because Bob doesn't like anybody brainy. When they're around Ronnie Hoa they talk about books, because Ronnie's really smart.

They try to be everything to everybody and after a while they almost forget what *they* were like in the first place.

What if you don't like yourself the way you are?

You *can* improve. But before you go kicking yourself around, remember that what you dislike today may not bother you at all tomorrow. The girl who detests wearing glasses may discover it's just not important later on. The boy who has never been good at baseball and wished for all the world that he was a better batter may find, when he's fifteen or sixteen, that he doesn't care at all about the game and has a whole new field of interest.

You will change. You can count on that. And so will some of your ideas about what you want to become or do or accomplish.

"But I always seem to do such dumb things," one girl said, in talking about herself. "Why am *I* always the one who stands up to give a report and forgets what she's going to say? Why am *I* always the one who falls off my bike in front of the supermarket?"

Don't look now, but you're not alone. Every day, in every way, other kids are making mistakes too. And while you go on forever and ever remembering yours and feeling embarrassed by them, others have long since forgotten *your* goofs and are busy remembering their own.

If you were perfect, think how uncomfortable others would be around you. The only reason they laughed when you dropped your tray in the lunchroon was because they were so glad it was you and not them. Whenever you goof, it reminds other people that they are not alone, so look on the bright side.

Maybe you *like* being different. Maybe you want to be so different from everybody else that people actually turn and stare as you walk by.

You don't really have to go to all that trouble. You are different and special too. You don't have to work at it—just be yourself—whatever that is.

GETTING ACQUAINTED

Now that you've had practice describing your friends, write a little paragraph about yourself. Take a good look in a full-length mirror. What do you really look like? How do you dress? What things do you like to do? What things do you dislike? What are your faults? What are your talents? Include whatever comes to mind, no matter how small it seems.

What do you look like on paper? Does your description sound like somebody you would want to get to know? Or somebody you would rather avoid?

Write a second paragraph about yourself. If you could become anything at all, what would you choose? How would you change yourself? What are the most important things in the world to you?

Compare what you are, and what you would like to be, with the descriptions you wrote of your friends. How many of them share your interests? How many of them would be glad to see you succeed in becoming the type of person you want to be? How do you really match up?

Sarah wrote that what she disliked most about her friend Lorie was the way she bossed people around. And yet, when she took a good look at herself, she had to admit that one of her own faults was bossiness.

Peter dislikes the fact that his friend Jack is often grumpy—always looking on the dark side of things. And yet, when Peter wrote a description of himself, he sounded a lot like Jack. Whenever one of his friends has a new idea, Peter is always the first to say, "It'll never work."

It's a fact that the things we most dislike about others are often faults we see in ourselves.

It's rather strange, but all of us have a

tendency to take the credit for the good things about us and blame someone else for our faults.

Jill says she does poorly in math because her mother always had a hard time with arithmetic.

David thinks he's shy because his mother says David's father never goes out of his way to be sociable.

Sandy says the reason she plays so badly in volleyball is that she's always chosen to be on the wrong team.

Dennis thinks he's fat because it runs in the family.

But when Jill and David and Sandy and Dennis get good grades on a test, they don't say it's because it runs in the family. They say it's because they studied hard. When they do well in soccer, they don't say it's because their parents were great in the game. They say it's because they've stayed in good form. When they all got special parts in the sixth grade play, they didn't give the credit to someone else. They said it was because they happened to do well at try-outs.

We are what we are because of a number of things. Partly it's because of our parents, partly it's because of what happens to us and what our experience has been, and partly it's because of what we ourselves do.

It may be that David's shyness, in part, *is* due to the fact that his father is shy, but then his grandfather might have been shy and his great-grandfather, too. There comes a time when we have to stop looking for somebody to blame and take it upon ourselves to change the pattern.

If people always take advantage of us and boss us around, it's partly because we let them. If people are always gossiping with us about someone else, it's partly because we encourage them. If we keep getting into trouble whenever we're with a certain friend, it's because we go along with it.

Things don't just happen to us. Each of us has a say in most matters. Only earthquakes and such can take us totally by surprise.

SHYNESS

Shyness really is a problem for some people, and whatever the cause, it's painful. Ask David. He'll tell you.

When David walks into a new classroom for the first time, or enter's someone's party, he wishes he could just crawl in unnoticed like a mouse and hide in a corner. He hates it when people are looking at him. His palms sweat when somebody asks him a question. If he could just be invisible, he thinks, how nice it would be.

But that's only part of the way he feels. If he had a choice, it would be to walk into the room like anybody else and not feel embarrassed; to go up to anybody at all and begin a conversation; to go anywhere he liked without feeling shaky because people were watching him. Nobody really wants to be shy. Shyness happens to be second choice.

We cannot say for sure why any one person is shy, because there are many different causes. Sometimes the parents are so shy that the child has never really learned how to get along socially. Sometimes the child has a handicap which makes him feel inferior. Sometimes he only *thinks* he has a handicap.

One of David's problems is that he has a distorted view of his friends. He is always looking at their successes and never at their faults. He doesn't even admit they have faults. All he sees is how clever they seem and how popular and attractive and wonderful. Compared to them, he believes, he's nothing.

Martha is shy because she has the strange notion that everybody knows what she is thinking and feeling without her ever having to tell them. And because people can only guess what is going on in Martha's head, they often guess wrong. Then Martha's feelings are hurt. Other people seem rude and inconsiderate to her, so she keeps even more to herself, which only makes the problem worse.

Gene is shy because he had some bad experiences as a small child. He began school when he was four, not five, and was not quite able to compete with the older children. Classmates can be cruel, and they used to tease him about the things he couldn't do. If he tipped over his chair or cut out his paper shamrock the wrong way or wore short pants to school when the others wore long, they made fun of him. Gene decided he was a cruddy little freak, and the only way he could keep himself from being hurt was to try to get through life without anybody seeing or hearing him. Many children have similar experiences and often get over them in time, but so far Gene has not been able to work through his problems.

Shyness, then, for all its causes and reasons, basically shows that a person is afraid of attracting attention to himself for fear of what others might discover. The truth is that what others would discover might be a very nice, attractive, able person—if they could only get close enough to become friends.

FAKES AND FRAUDS

Is what we feel about ourselves inside what we show to the world? Or do we wear a mask? It is not always shyness that holds us back. Sometimes it's because we want to be popular.

Don liked to draw. In fact, he liked to paint and sculpt and make things out of wire and wood as well. If there was something he could make with his hands, Don made it. He hoped to design cars someday. For the moment, however, his hobby was birds, and he loved to take a sketchpad outdoors and sketch the ones he saw near the feeder.

He quickly learned not to discuss his bird sketches. In third grade, after spring vacation, when the teacher asked the class how they had spent their time, all the other boys seemed to have different things to talk about. Charlie had done skateboarding and Duke had been to Disney World and Larry had gone to a pro basketball game, and when it came Don's turn to tell what he had done, somehow a sketchbook full of robins didn't seem like such a big deal, so he lied and said he'd been out camping with his father.

And once when Larry came over to Don's house, he saw the sketchbook of birds and made fun of it. From then on Don was very careful not to show it to any of his friends. The more he thought about it, the more sure he was that they would all laugh.

A new boy, Jonathan, moved into the neighborhood. He, too, kept his love of art to himself. Once, when he was painting on his back porch, Don came over, so he slipped his paper under the table. "What are you doing?" Don had asked. "Nothing," he'd answered. "Just fooling around."

Don and Jonathan became friends, but they never talked about drawing and painting. Instead, they talked about soccer, which they didn't much like, and wrestling, which they hated but pretended to like, and each tried to be what he thought the other boy wanted him to be.

One day Jonathan invited Don up to his room and Don saw a sketch he'd made of a castle, with his name in the corner. Then Jonathan finally admitted that yes, he did like to draw now and then. And Don admitted that, well, he sort of liked to fool around, too.

All the next summer they spent constructing out of toothpicks and popsickle sticks the same castle Jonathan had drawn.

They ended up painting a mural for the all-purpose room at school the next fall. Every so often they talked about why they had tried to hide their real interests from each other and regretted the fun they had missed.

Sure, you may think, it's easy to be honest about your talents, your good points, but what about the rest? Do you really think you should go up to somebody and say, "Look, I don't brush my teeth as much as I should and my table manners are lousy and I've got this toe on my right foot that's really ugly?" Should a person be so honest about his bad points that he goes around advertising them?

Not advertising them, maybe, but you don't have to think they're a deep dark secret to be hidden forever from your friends. If you can't change them, ignore them. If you can't ignore them, laugh at them.

Your friends will regard them exactly as you do. If you've got a mole on your cheek and you go around half your life covering it up with your hand, everyone you meet will be dying to see what's under there. If, when somebody asks you about it (and it's none of their business, but people *do* ask rude questions), you blush and look away and mumble something about how unlucky you were to be born with this terrible thing, they will cringe and wince and agree that yes, the mole is ugly.

But if you accept the fact that this is you, and that there's a lot more to you than your mole—if you can say laughingly, "Yeah, it's my little buddy. Goes everywhere with me,"—they'll laugh too, and forget about it.

Perhaps you aren't an A student, but you get along well with your teachers. Perhaps you will never be a great athlete, but you can sure play the trumpet. You need to be as honest about your abilities as you are about the things you don't do as well. Once you begin to feel good about yourself in some ways, the others don't seem as important.

Look around you—the president of your student council, the principal of your school, your swimming instructor, your Scout leader—are they *all* handsome and attractive? Do they *always* say the right thing? Are they *always* even-tempered, fair, and intelligent?

Of course not. Everybody has imperfections. Everybody has problems. And you're no exception. They've got a lot more going for them than their looks, and so have you.

How we feel about ourselves may not be the way we are coming across to other people. We may think that we are friendly and kind and thoughtful, but others may have a far different impression of us. And that's where a lot of problems develop with friends.

We may know that someone does not like us, but we may not know why. We realize that other people seem defensive when we are around, but we don't understand what makes them act that way.

Learning to see ourselves as others see us is the next step in becoming acquainted with who we really are.

CHAPTER 3

AS OTHERS SEE US

MIRRORS MAY NOT HELP

While it's important to take a good look at ourselves, we can never really see ourselves as others see us. We can only guess.

Even if you walked up to your very best friend and said, "I want you to tell me honestly how I look to you, how I act," your friend might have a hard time doing so.

Even if our friends are perfectly honest, they can only tell us how we seem to them, not to everyone else. And if they are like most good friends, they don't want to hurt our feelings.

Down deep, they may know that we eat spaghetti like a pig, and grunt over our food in the lunchroom, but they'll never tell us that.

47

They'll probably say, instead, with some embarrassment, "Well, truthfully, your table manners could be improved."

And the next time we eat with them in the lunchroom we'll wonder just what they meant. We'll make sure we take a napkin and that we don't wipe our fingers on our jeans, but we'll go right on slurping spaghetti like a pig and grunting over our food, thinking we're doing fine.

We could, of course, ask our *enemies* what they think about us, but they'd have so much fun telling us that we don't want to give them that pleasure.

To really see ourselves as others see us, we have to understand what people actually mean by the words they say and try to guess at what they've left out. Like detectives, we have to look for clues in the way they act toward us or by reading the expressions on their faces. It's like learning a new kind of language.

LIGHTS, CAMERA, ACTION

One good way to see ourselves as others see us is to notice how people act when we are around.

48

When you approach a group of friends who are talking together on the playground, how do they react? Do they stop talking or change the subject, as though they can't really share their thoughts with you?

When you sit down at a table of friends in the lunchroom who had been quietly talking before you came, do they become loud and silly because you are there?

Do other people begin teasing you as soon as you arrive? Bossing you, perhaps? Worse yet, do they ignore you? Or does the group go right on being themselves, discussing whatever they were talking about before you came, laughing at whatever they thought was funny? You'll know if there is a slight change in the atmosphere when you arrive. It may not be anything you can put your finger on, but you'll know.

Danny was late getting to the lunchroom. The teacher had kept him for a few minutes to rewrite a paper he had written sloppily. When he got his tray and approached a table of classmates, they were discussing the movie they had seen in science that morning.

As soon as they saw Danny, however, one yelled, "Heeeey, look who finally made it! Put 'er there, Danny boy!" and held out his hand with a marshmallow cookie concealed in the palm. Danny gave the hand a slap and the cookie went sailing over the table and landed on the ham sandwich of somebody seated at the next table.

This produced a volley of paper straws blown from the second table, and Danny himself retaliated by picking up a not-quite-empty milk carton and skidding it across the floor.

It was at that moment that the lunchroom supervisor descended upon the table and scolded, "Danny Peters, why is it that everything is orderly until you arrive? Why is it that every day, no matter where you're sitting, your table seems to get into trouble?"

"I didn't start it!" Danny said defensively, and he was half right. But there was something about Danny and his past reputation that signaled the others to goof off.

George has the opposite problem. He has been trying to make more friends, and each day he chooses a different table in the lunchroom so he will get to know all the other boys better.

He usually sits where there seems to be laughter and interesting talk, trying his best to be sociable, but somehow it never quite works out.

Only yesterday he sat down beside Steve and Gary because he really likes them. They said hi, made room for him, and nobody was unfriendly.

This time, George thought, *I'm going to fit in.*

The boys had been talking about roller coasters, and when Gary told about a new one he'd seen that went sixty miles an hour, George told them about one that went seventy miles an hour.

When Steve mentioned a ride he had been on that turned him upside down, George told them about the one he'd been on last year that had turned him upside down, and spun him around.

The lunch hour was scarcely half over when George knew that, for some reason, he was turning the boys off. He thought he was being friendly and contributing to the conversation. He did not see that much of the time he was simply topping whatever anybody else said. He was not bragging especially, but topping them nonetheless.

Do you bring out the best in other people when you are around them? Do you give them an equal chance to talk? Do you show as much enthusiasm and response to stories they tell you as they show for your own?

Some people work so hard around others trying to be entertaining and witty and clever that they cannot understand why they still seem to have no really close friends. Don't others always laugh at their jokes? Don't they seem to enjoy their stories?

Everybody wants to be listened to. Nobody wants to be simply an admiring friend, entertained all the time by you. Each of us wants to be recognized as an interesting person in our own right, and we want the chance to hold center stage occasionally, too.

BY HOOK OR CROOK

Some people don't make friends at all; they only think they do.

Don't they always get their own way? Don't others usually do what they want them to do? Doesn't that mean they are popular?

No. It might mean that they use other people, that they trick them, perhaps, without ever realizing it, into giving them what they want.

Some people get their own way by pure and simple bossiness, because their voices are louder or they make such a fuss.

Ray always gets to be on the team he chooses. He usually is first up to bat. When he loses a point in table tennis, he often gets to play it over. But not because he is liked, not because he is right; it is simply that he makes so much noise and carries on an argument for so long over such small things that the others get tired of listening to him. They would rather give in than spend fifteen minutes arguing with him.

Ray thinks he is popular, but he doesn't realize nobody's glad to have him around. He doesn't know of all the parties and trips he has missed because people would rather not invite him.

Gail also gets her way, and she is far from bossy. She's rather soft spoken. In fact, she can get her way by not saying anything at all. It's the way she looks, the way she shrugs, the way she presses her lips together.

"How about being in charge of publicity?" someone will ask her when the Girl Scouts are planning a banquet.

A look of disappointment crosses Gail's face, and she says nothing.

"Okay, Gail? That okay with you?" Sandra asks her.

Gail sighs and looks at the floor.

"Well, what do you *want* to do?" Sandra asks.

"If you've forgotten already, . . ." Gail pouts, a hurt look in her eyes.

"Forgotten what?"

"I thought it was agreed I could do the decorations."

"We told Elsie she could do them."

Again the hurt look, the eyes on the floor, the lips pressed together.

"Well, if you don't think I'm good enough . . ." Gail continues, as though on the verge of tears.

"Oh, for heaven's sake, I don't care," Elsie

says. "Let her do the decorations. I'll take publicity."

Gail won again by making the others feel guilty. She won the project, at least, but she didn't win any popularity over it.

Both Ray and Gail are manipulators—people who get their own way by slowly, carefully, wearing others down or tricking them by some means.

It does not say very much about you as a friend if this is the way you treat others. A person should be able to ask openly and directly for what he wants without resorting to games or lies or manipulation.

If Ray really thought it fair that he be on a certain team or that he play a serve over, he should have said so openly and simply. If the majority of the boys did not agree, then he should have accepted their opinion.

If Gail really believed that she had been promised the job of decorations, she should have said so plainly without playing on the others' feelings.

Just getting what you want may not get you very far in the long run.

WHAT ABOUT BULLIES?

Almost every grownup remembers a bully from childhood. Almost every child has met one. There doesn't seem to be a school or a playground or a neighborhood without them. Nobody likes a bully, and yet they keep popping up.

What makes a bully? All kinds of things. The bully may have an older brother or a dad who knocks him around, so he takes it out on others. He may be unsure of his own popularity, so he bosses and teases other kids in an effort to impress his classmates. He may feel definitely inferior to people his own age, and it makes him feel important to order younger ones around. Or he may be really disturbed inside himself and get some kind of pleasure out of frightening or even hurting other children. Girls can be bullies as well as boys.

But one thing is sure: bullies usually pick on people they feel they can beat. You rarely see a bully attacking anybody older or bigger or even the same size.

What you can do about a bully depends on

how bad the teasing gets. If it is just words he uses, making faces and calling names, the best thing to do is ignore him or laugh it off. He only does it to upset you, and if you don't react, he will probably leave you alone.

It may still make you angry inside, and you may still like very much to bop him in the nose, but you're only asking for more trouble if you react with anger. Ignoring him will probably cure him. Think about why he teases, and perhaps you won't feel as angry at him.

If the bullying is more threatening than mere teasing, such as throwing your cap up in a tree or grabbing the swing away from you, you might try ignoring it and going somewhere else. If it is something you can't ignore, you could say, "Why don't you grow up?" If you treat the bully as somebody really childish, he may be embarrassed and stop it.

If his behavior is definitely aggressive—if he shoves you off the swing or knocks you down on the sidewalk, the problem becomes more difficult. What you do will depend partly on what you have been taught by your parents.

Some parents say that the only way to treat a

bully is to give him a taste of his own medicine. If he punches you in the mouth, punch him back. Even though you are smaller, they say, and are likely to get the worst of the deal, if he's going to hit you regardless you might as well defend yourself.

Other parents say that you should never resort to violence. Persons should be able to solve their problems without fighting.

There are cases where each method seems to work. Lloyd, for example, had become the object of teasing from a big boy named Russ. Last year it had been somebody else and the year before that, still another person, but this year it was Lloyd that Russ had chosen to pick on.

Russ followed him home from school each day and tried to step on the back of Lloyd's sneakers. If he ate an apple, he always threw the core at Lloyd. If Lloyd was sitting on the steps and Russ wanted to go up, he simply stepped on Lloyd.

Lloyd had tried ignoring him, but as the weeks went on, he got angrier and the teasing got worse.

Then one day Lloyd was out riding bikes with his younger brother Johnny. Johnny had just learned to ride. Lloyd was following along behind to make sure he was all right. Suddenly Russ stood up from behind a bush and let fly a handful of walnuts. He was aiming for Lloyd, but some of them hit Johnny, who fell off his bike.

In an instant, Lloyd leaped off his bike, lunged at Russ, and knocked him to the ground, hitting him hard with his fists. He was so angry he just didn't care any more that Russ was bigger.

Russ was so taken by surprise that he didn't have time to respond. He managed to whack Lloyd a time or two, but a moment later the fight was over, and Lloyd got back on his bike beside Johnny and rode away.

Russ has said a few choice words to Lloyd since then, but he has not touched him. In this instance, fighting back seemed to work.

But Russ had another run-in with someone else in the neighborhood, a young boy named Brian. He teased Brian in the same way, pushed him around, and tried to make him lose his temper.

One day, when a group of children were coming home from school and came to a large mud puddle on the corner, Russ edged over to where Brian was walking, stuck out his foot, and tripped him. Then, catching him off-balance, he shoved him into the puddle.

As the other children watched uneasily, Russ leaned against a tree laughing as Brian stood up, dripping and dirty. Nobody spoke. Friends stood around uncomfortably wondering what Brian would do, and even Russ stopped laughing to see what would happen.

Brian didn't touch him. He didn't threaten. Slowly he shook the water from his coat, wiped off his hands, and turned to Russ.

"What's your problem, Russ?" he asked coldly. "You sick or something? Do you get your kicks out of knocking other people around? How old are you, anyway? Three?"

"Yeah, Russ," the other children said when they saw there would be no fight. "What's wrong with you?" And they turned their backs on him and walked on down the street with Brian.

Russ did not bother Brian again, and Brian's parents said that he had done the right thing.

It's good to enlist the help of your friends. If a bully knows he has an appreciative audience, he's going to be tempted to put on a show. But if he knows that people are going to turn against him, it won't be so inviting.

If at all possible, try to handle the problem yourself—you and your friends—without asking a parent or teacher to help you. There will be times, however, when it is necessary to ask for help.

If a bully has been threatening you or actually doing you physical harm, or if the threats become so scary that you are no longer playing at a certain playground or going to a particular park, then an adult should be asked to step in.

Your father or uncle or a neighbor might be willing to go to the parents of the bully for a heart-to-heart talk. Sometimes the bully's parents have no idea what their child is doing and will put a stop to it at once. If there is violence involved—if the bully carries a jackknife, for example—it may be that a police officer will pay a visit to the house.

Dealing with bullies is not easy, and it's scary. But if you can learn to handle the problem with words whenever possible, you will have learned something very valuable. You will meet many people in your life who disagree with you and take advantage of you, and you can't go on forever punching them in the mouth. If you can learn to say the right thing in the right way, you will gain respect from all who know you.

LOSING FRIENDS BY BEING TOO FRIENDLY

It sounds rather strange, but it happens. Sometimes persons want so much to be our friends that their very eagerness seems to sound an alarm.

What's the matter? some little voice says down deep inside us. *If someone works that hard to get friends, there must be something wrong.*

We have all known boys or girls who were

not very popular and tried to buy others' friendship by giving out money at school or coming to the lunchroom with extra sweets to give to others.

That is always sad to see. No one should have to try to buy another's friendship. Friendship can't be bought. People may be polite to you because you have just given them something, but it does not make them respect you any more. They may not even like you better for it.

There are many ways people use to protect themselves from being rejected. Some people, instead of giving out candy, give out compliments. They try to make friends by flattering them. They choose the person they most admire and lavish him or her with praise.

Linda was such a person. Her ideal was Joni Valrugo, and every day she had a new compliment for Joni.

"I like your hair, Joni," she'd say, even though Joni's hair looked the same as it had the day before.

"I like your jeans, Joni." "I like your bracelet,

Joni." "Your report was great." "Your picture was beautiful."

Everybody likes compliments. Everyone wants to know when he or she does something well or looks especially nice.

But after a while Joni began to suspect that Linda was not sincere. As the compliments continued day after day, they lost their importance, and actually began to irritate her. Linda could not understand what was wrong with her campaign to become Joni's friend. Wasn't she being especially nice? Wasn't she being complimentary? What was wrong with that?

Sometimes it seems easier to use a gimmick to get someone to like us than to change the things about ourselves which are unlikable. Candy and nickels and smiles and compliments are only gimmicks.

Other people protect themselves from possible rejection by rejecting, or insulting, others first. Wayne seemed to have been born with a smile on his face and his foot in his mouth. He felt he could say anything at all, no matter how insulting, if he pretended it was a joke. He was known as the practical joker, the tease, with a remark for every occasion. If it weren't for the smile on his face, somebody would have pasted him one in the mouth long ago. It's hard to argue with someone who says he's only kidding. "What's the matter, can't take a joke?" Wayne always said when somebody got annoyed with him.

Someone finally told him off. Somebody finally took him aside and told him what he was doing to other people and how it was coming across to them. And though Wayne didn't want to hear it, and was angry, he had to admit, after thinking it over, that they were right.

But habits are hard to change. Wayne soon discovered that when he kept his joking comments to himself, he didn't have much left to say. He realized that his joking had been a defense—a way of cutting down other people because he felt inferior himself. He had, however, chosen a very cowardly way to do it.

He soon found that he could still be clever and witty by turning his barbed comments upon himself. Gradually, as Wayne checked his teasing and kidding, he sensed that the others were happier to have him around.

Some people have a difficult time accepting silences. Whenever there is a lull in the conversation, they feel uncomfortable and rush to fill it up with words—anything at all, as long as it breaks the dreaded quiet.

There is nothing wrong with silence. Good friends who are comfortable with each other can sit on the porch swing for a long time just rocking, each in his own thoughts. People can eat together, enjoying their food, without filling the empty spaces in conversation with noise.

People who talk just to be talking often are not only annoying, but sometimes say things on the spur of the moment they would not have said if they weren't in such a hurry to say *something*. Instead of a simple hi, they blurt out, "Boy, you meet all kinds of people on this street!"

Keep your personality honest. You don't really have to make a witty remark every time you open your mouth. If you have to disguise your true self, your mask will soon wear thin.

If you feel *compelled* to break the silence, if a

simple hi is not your style yet you always say the wrong thing, try a compliment—something like, "I hear you did very well in try-outs yesterday." But be sure it's sincere.

We cannot *make* other people like us. We cannot force anyone to be our friend. Friendship is a two-way street. And sometimes, it is just as important to know how to disagree or argue with others as it is to know how to be pleasant.

CHAPTER 4

QUARRELING WITH CARE

PEOPLE, NOT PUPPETS

It's a fact that no matter how kind, thoughtful, or interesting you are, not everybody is going to like you.

Because of differences in personalities, interests, and backgrounds, there will always be some people it just seems impossible to be close to, and the best you can hope for in those cases is to remain polite with each other.

As for friends, you can't expect them to agree with you all the time either. You can't expect them to like everything you like or feel the same way about an experience or even want to be with you all the time. Nor can anyone expect this of you.

Sometimes this comes as a shock. Paul and Bob found themselves in the same classroom on the first day of school. They had not known each other before, but after six weeks, they were both pleased to discover that they had a lot in common.

They both collected matchbook covers, both liked to tinker with their bikes, both were Scouts, and both liked camping and model building. It got to the point where, although they'd never really discussed it, they each assumed that what one liked, the other liked.

When they were out riding bikes one day then, it came as a surprise when Bob mentioned that he was going to enroll in a gymnastics course at the Y.

"Gymnastics?" choked Paul. "That dumb stuff? I wouldn't take gymnastics if somebody paid me a million dollars!"

It was a surprise to Bob as well. He had just assumed that Paul would be interested—might even want to join up too, in fact. Neither boy seemed able to accept the fact that in spite of the many interests they shared, they were still two individuals.

How can you get your friends to accept you? It's important, from the very beginning, to be honest about what you are like and what your interests are.

Then you must be sure that you, in turn, respect other people's interests, no matter how different they might be from yours. You may care nothing about hermit crabs, but if one of your friends enjoys hermit crabs and likes to talk about them now and then, it would be pretty thoughtless to tell him you think crabs make stupid pets.

There is a difference between lively, good-natured debate and destructive criticism. If your friend, who is not particularly interested in snorkeling, pays attention when you talk about it and asks questions, he expects the same attention and courtesy from you when he talks about his hermit crab.

If, however, he tries to get you to buy one, you have every right to tell him, as politely as you can, that hermit crabs aren't your thing, and there are other ways you'd rather spend your money.

If, in spite of that, he tries to talk you into it

and is interested in your objections, then you are perfectly free to tell them to him. Be sure you talk about the pets themselves, not the kind of people who like them.

If you say, "I just can't get that excited about a little animal running around from shell to shell," you have told him honestly how you feel about crabs, and you have not attacked him.

On the other hand, you have insulted him if you say, "Hermit crabs are for weirdos, man! People who would choose a crab over a cat or dog must have something wrong with them,"

WHAT CAN YOU EXPECT OF A REAL FRIEND?

It is hard to imagine two people being friends without ever disagreeing. If you and your friend never argue, never see things in a different way, it is because one of you is not being honest.

Differences aside, however, what can you expect from people who say they are your friends?

1. You should be able to count on them to

stick by you in rough times as well as smooth times. If they were all working hard to help you get elected as treasurer of your sixth grade class, you would expect real friends to stay by you even if you lost. And if you accomplish something special, you should be able to count on their friendship, too, without their becoming jealous.

2. You should expect a real friend to be loyal. If Ed tells you he thinks your Halloween party is a great idea, it would hurt to find out later he had been telling other kids that he thinks it's silly and childish. If he really feels you are making a mistake, a friend should be honest with you and tell you as politely as possible.

3. A good friend should be dependable. If Sue says she will lend you her long cape for your part in the school play and then changes her mind the night before the performance, she has proved herself to be—in this instance —unreliable.

4. Good friends should go out of their way occasionally to help you. Friendship is rarely 50/50. Rather it is a constantly shifting balance.

Gloria and Bernice were such friends. Some of the time the balance between needing and giving was 50/50. Gloria needed help in math, and Bernice gave it to her; Bernice needed help in English, and Gloria gave it to her. Bernice was better in tennis; Gloria was better in volleyball. They enjoyed being able to help each other.

One time, however, when Gloria's cat was attacked and killed by a large German shepherd, Gloria went through several weeks of sadness. She felt very bad about everything, especially herself, since she had neglected to take the cat indoors when she saw that the large dog was loose. For some time she seemed moody, uninterested in hobbies the girls had previously shared, and Bernice had to work hard to pull her out of it. For that brief period, Bernice was doing all the giving and Gloria was contributing very little to the relationship.

And yet the experience made them even better friends. Gloria had found that Bernice could be counted on even when things were not going well. And a few months later, when some of the girls in the chorus were selected to give a performance at the state capital and Gloria, but not Bernice, was chosen to go, it was Gloria's turn to be kind and understanding. She was as loyal and friendly as ever; she did not talk about the trip all the time and focused, instead, on the things that she and Bernice could share.

Remember that even though good friends are all these things, they are not all of these things all the time. They do make mistakes. They even hurt us. But forgiving is part of friendship, too.

KEEPING IT POLITE

When you have to disagree, it is how you go about it and what you say that's important. Consider the following statements:

1. "Marcie, I'm not sure that Pat would like this tennis book for her birthday. Maybe we can think of something better."

2. "Not a tennis book, Marcie! Can't you do better than that?"

3. "A tennis book! Are you out of your mind, Marcie? Pat can't even play dodge ball, much less tennis!"

4. "This is absolutely the stupidest present I ever saw, Marcie. Don't you ever pay attention to what other people like? That's you, all right—going off and buying the first thing you see."

When someone has something unpleasant to say to you, how do you like to be told?

If you're getting ready to have something out with a friend, to let your feelings fly, decide in advance what your purpose is. Which of these statements best expresses what you want to do?

1. "I'm furious, and I'm going to insult him just like he insulted me."

2. "Her argument is ridiculous. When I get through with this, she's going to look like an idiot."

3. "I'm positive I'm right. If I could just make him see my point of view. . . ."

4. "He has very strong feelings about this, and so do I. If we can just get things out in the open and clear the air. . . ."

Chances are there's a little bit of everything mixed up in your feelings. If an argument is brewing, you've probably got some hurtful, angry feelings against the other person, even if he is, or was, your best friend. You also want to get even. And possibly there's the real wish to patch things up, to understand and be understood.

If your main objective is to humiliate and hurt, you will pick the sharpest sword you can find and go after him while his back is turned. You will pick the choicest, meanest words possible to use, and, being his exfriend, you probably know all the weak points, so you can attack him right between the eyes with what you say.

If he ever told you that he still gets homesick when he's away from home, you'll throw that in too, in front of everybody else, even though it may have nothing whatever to do with the argument. And of course you'll pick a public place so he will be embarrassed before the very people he would least like to have watch.

If your main objective is to change the situation—to resolve the quarrel and keep his friendship—you will choose a place that is private and a time when neither of you are hurried.

You will stick to the problem at hand and not

bring in all the other things you can think of to keep the fires burning. If the quarrel is about the way he talks about you behind your back, don't tell him his ears are ugly too.

If you really hope, once the argument is over, that you will understand each other better and become friends once more, you will not back him into a corner. You will not say, "Either you buy the food for the campout, Pete, or you don't go. Everybody else has had a turn." Pete may pick up his backpack and go home, and that would be the last thing you wanted.

Provide alternatives. If Pete, for some reason, detests grocery shopping, assign him KP duty instead and relieve somebody else who hates washing pots and pans. It's not fair, of course, to let Pete get away with having all the easy jobs while the others do the hard work, but if it's a particular job that seems to be causing so much trouble, and he's willing to take another equally icky chore, then that should work well. It's important to know when to give in a little and when to stick to principles.

The single, most important thing you can do when you are having a quarrel with someone is to put your feelings on the line—all of them—just as honestly as you can and encourage the other person to do the same.

Some people do an excellent job of telling another person exactly how they feel, in big words and colorful phrases, and then, as the other stares, limp and awed—trying to get his own counterattack in order—the first person leaves the room or changes the subject or simply concludes that the argument is over, that nothing more need be said.

Say exactly what is on your mind and wait for a response. If Cathy said she couldn't go bowling with you the night before because she was sick, and you found out later she went to a movie with Sharon, go up to Cathy when she is alone and say quite simply, "Cathy, you told me you were sick last night, and I heard you went to a movie with Sharon. That really hurt. How come?"

You have not accused her of being disloyal. You have not called her names. You told her honestly what you heard, what you felt, and asked for her own explanation. You have been honest, open, and—more than that—strong enough to put your feelings on the line.

You could have ignored her for a whole week and never answered when she spoke to you.

You could have passed her in the hall and asked snidely, "How are you *feeling*, Cathy? Yeah, you were real sick last night, weren't you?"

You could have confronted her in the cafeteria and told her she was a two-faced liar.

Instead, you gave her a chance to reply, and there's always the possibility she *might* have had a reasonable explanation. She may tell you truthfully that she's a terrible bowler and didn't want to embarrass herself—that she didn't have the nerve to admit it.

Even if there *is* no good answer, even if she was disloyal and unthinking, you have proved yourself to be honest and straightforward, and she can't help but admire that.

AN ARGUMENT HAS TWO SIDES

This is something we all know, but are likely to forget in the heat of battle. We are so busy thinking of good arguments for our side that we scarcely even hear what the other

person has to say. If we take time to really listen, however, we will usually discover that things aren't quite as good or bad as they seem.

Following are some common quarrels that arise between friends. Perhaps, in some of them, it will seem quite obvious to you who is right and who is wrong. In others, it will not seem very clear at all. How would you work out these problems?

Choosing What to Do

Pamela: "Whenever Jane and I get together, it seems we always end up doing what she wants. The other day, for example, I brought over my skateboard but she didn't want to do that. I suggested volleyball and table tennis, but we finally ended up playing Monopoly, which I hate."

Jane: "The problem is the only things Pam ever suggests are things she does well. She knows I'm awful at sports, but that's all she ever suggests."

In Groups of Three

Ted: "Keith and I get along okay together when there's just the two of us, but as soon as somebody else comes along, there's trouble. I always have the feeling that Keith and the other guy are taking sides against me, and that makes me mad."

Keith: "When I'm with Ted, he acts insulted if I want anybody else along. He even seems hurt if I ask someone to sit with us in the lunchroom. I like Ted, but I don't enjoy being alone with him *all* the time."

Reliability

Nat: "I use to like Billy, but I can't trust him. He tells me he'll be over on Saturday, and then he never shows up. Or he says he'll save me a seat on the bus, and then he sits with somebody else."

Billy: "The trouble with Nat is he's always trying to pin me down. He'll ask if I can come over on Saturday, and I'll say, 'Probably, if I get all my work done.' Then, if I don't get it done and don't go, he gets angry, even though it was not a promise."

Speaking Up

Janice: "Corrine is really a coward. Once a bunch of us were going to talk to the teacher about the big assignments she gives us over the weekends. Corrine had been complaining about the assignments like everybody else, but she wouldn't go with us. She was afraid we'd get into trouble. She lets other people do the dirty work."

Corrine: "Janice's mouth is going to get her in big trouble some day. It's almost as though she goes around looking for trouble. One day she got some girls together and they went over to Betsy's house to tell her why she was unpopular at school. Can you imagine having a bunch of girls come up to you and tell you why nobody likes you? She talks before she thinks."

Helping with Homework

Polly: "Greg is really conceited when it comes to school work. He does well in science, and that's a hard subject for me. Sometimes I just don't understand the assigment, but when I call and ask him to explain it to me, he makes a big deal out of it, as though I wasn't paying attention. Can't he realize that no one can be smart in everything?"

Greg: "The problem is that a lot of the time

Polly doesn't just want to know how to do something, she wants me to work it out for her. If I end up giving her the answer when she hasn't really worked for it, that's not fair."

Secrets

Jennifer: "When Lorraine's around, she seems like the nicest person in the world. You can't help but want to tell her things, she's so sympathetic and understanding. But too many times I've told her something and found out later that six other kids know about it. If she was really loyal, she wouldn't go telling my secrets"

Lorraine: "I'm never sure when Jennifer wants me to tell somebody something or not. Once when she told me she liked Nancy's brother, I had the feeling that down underneath she really wanted me to tell Nancy so her brother would find out. But Jennifer got mad when I did."

WINNING AND LOSING

You have probably heard the saying that it is possible to win an argument and lose your friend. The whole point of winning is to stay friends—to win your friend over to your point of view.

Everyone likes a good loser, but if your friend is a poor loser it may be in part because you are being a poor winner. If you do happen to win your argument, do it gracefully. If possible, don't even let the other person know you've won. With practice, you can reach an agreement without pounding your chest and bellowing about it. "I told you so" is one of the worst things you can say.

Being a good loser is more difficult. It's hard, sometimes, to be polite when you feel so rotten inside. Some losers try to make the other person feel guilty or make some kind of extra demand, as though the winner owes them something.

Learning to apologize is one of the hardest, but most useful, lessons you can learn. You don't have to get down on your knees or cry or call yourself names. Just a simple, "Hey, Jim, you were right. I just wasn't thinking," is enough. Or, "Marlene, I'm sorry about what I said yesterday. I wasn't feeling like myself."

Some people find it difficult being a leader. They seem to work well on committees when somebody else is directing a project, but as soon as they're put in charge, something happens. They begin barking out commands and ordering people around. They can't seem to accept authority gracefully.

The secret of being a good leader or director or president or chairman is to bring out the best in other people. You want them to know that they are important, that they can contribute, that their ideas are worth considering. Nobody likes to rattle around doing nothing.

Maybe you *are* a very capable person. Maybe you can play the piano better than anyone else or draw better posters or come up with the best ideas for a program. But if you end up doing everything yourself, it becomes a one-man show, and the others might as well go home.

A leader knows the value of seeing that everyone has a job to do and that each person is praised for that job. Sometimes he only *thinks* that he can do it better himself, and is surprised to find out how talented others are when given a chance.

CHAPTER 5

CHANGING

ALWAYS IS AN AWFULLY LONG TIME

You have probably heard somebody say that the only thing you can really count on is change.

When we meet friends we like very much, it is natural to wish that they would be our friends forever and ever. Possibly they will be.

Sometimes it is not just one person, but a group of friends you have had a lot of fun with and with whom you have so much in common. You wonder why the group can't go on forever.

But forever is a very long time. Families move away, other families move in, situations change, groups change, people change, and friendships change. Adults who decide to marry—who have thought about it a long time—hope that their love will last forever, but forever is a lot to ask of friends.

When two friends have had many good times together, or a group of friends have enjoyed things together, it can be sad when they sense that things are changing—that one of the friends is no longer as interested as she used to be or that someone has a new hobby which is taking up most of his time.

Some people become very upset when friends begin to drift away and try to hold them back. They may get angry and accuse the other person of liking another friend better. Or they may try to make the person feel guilty because he or she is no longer as interested in the friendship.

Neither way will work. If they continue to do things with us merely because they don't like to see us angry or hurt, that is not the kind of friendship we really want. No one likes to feel he has to bribe or threaten or trick somebody into spending time with him.

No one belongs to anyone else. People who marry make a commitment to each other, but neither is a possession of the other. Friends are not possessions, either. We do not own them, and we do not belong to any one person. We should all be able to have as many friends as we wish.

Some friends we will like very much, more than anyone else, and others—while we enjoy being around them—may not seem as close to us. But it is good to have many different kinds of friends.

Sometimes people feel very close to each other for awhile, and then they seem to move apart. Sometimes this is only temporary. Perhaps they just need a breathing spell from each other. When school opens again, or something else brings them back together, they are still good friends, sometimes better than they were before.

Other times the break is more or less permanent, and although they may still be friendly toward each other, they never again become the close pals they once were.

Even though you may lose your very best friend, it's not the only best friend you will ever have. It is not so much a particular person we like, but a *type* of person, and there are many people of that type, whatever it is.

When Kevin moved away, Benny thought he would never have such a good friend again. He and Kevin seemed to like the same things, make the same grades, and read the same books. Kevin was sort of quiet, but funny, and he could make Benny laugh in ways that nobody else could.

And yet, in the year that followed, Benny met a number of other boys who were quiet like Kevin, had a sense of humor like Kevin, and liked many of the things that he and Kevin had done together. None of them *were* Kevin, but then Kevin could never be one of them either, and some of them had talents that Kevin didn't have.

It is always sad when a friend leaves us for what we feel to be a poor reason. When Marie's father died, her best friend, Katherine, stopped coming over. She always had an excuse—she didn't feel well or she had to go to the library—and finally Marie stopped asking.

It seemed especially cruel to Marie, who was struggling with her grief over her father, to lose

Katherine, too. But she finally found out from other friends that death was something difficult for Katherine to accept. Katherine did not like to talk about it or think about it or be around anybody who reminded her of it. She knew she would be ill at ease around Marie and possibly say the wrong thing. And so she solved it in her own way by not coming around at all.

Sometimes friends leave us because some member of our family gets into trouble. Sometimes they leave us because we can't afford the things that they can buy or because we are having a particularly hard time in school or for some other reason.

This always hurts, because we know then that they were only "fair-weather" friends, and that when times are stormy, they go to somebody else.

There is no one good way to get friends to come back or to like us again. If it is something we have done of course—a thoughtless remark or act—it is up to us to apologize and set things right if we can.

But sometimes the only thing we can do is go on being ourselves, hoping that in time the friend will think it over and want to be friends again.

It is useless to keep after someone who does not *want* to be our friend. It is even worse to try to pretend we are somebody we aren't—to try to change our own personalities and interests just to capture the friendship of someone else. We are what we are, and if one particular person does not like us, there are others who will.

Mark had a different problem. He had recently moved to Illinois from Ohio and was eager to make new friends.

One of the first boys he met in his neighborhood was Jerry. Mark liked soccer and Jerry liked soccer. Mark liked pepperoni pizza and so did Jerry. Both boys had ten-speed bikes and both had younger brothers, and because Mark wanted a friend so badly, he told himself that Jerry was just the buddy he was looking for.

But in some ways—important ways—the boys were very different. Jerry disliked school, and he said so often. His attitude, in fact, was to get by with doing as little work as possible, by every trick imaginable. He also took money from his parents without their knowledge and spent it on sodas and doughnuts after school.

At first Mark tried telling himself that Jerry was just a fun-loving guy, a joker, and laughed off the things he did. But as the weeks went on, Mark realized that some of the things couldn't be laughed off—some were really serious. Jerry was not the type of close friend that Mark had been pretending he was. What was more, in going around with only Jerry, Mark was getting a reputation himself as sort of a troublemaker, and turning off some other boys who were more like him.

Gradually, Mark began spending more time with the other boys and less with Jerry. He found other friends he liked better. He was glad he had not waited too long to make the break, even though it meant spending some pretty lonely weekends by himself.

Sometimes friends do not want to break off with us, they just don't want to be with us as much as we want to be with them. Everyone has his own needs for privacy. Some people seem to need a lot of time by themselves—they enjoy doing things alone—and other people seem to need very little. This is a personal matter, and no one can decide it for anyone else.

You may think that Sharon would be better off if she went out more with friends, but she may not think so. She may have many hobbies, or projects, which interest her and find the time she spends alone exciting and worthwhile.

Being a good friend to someone else means accepting them as they are—including their right to be alone or to be with friends other than ourselves. And very often, after a weekend alone or with another friend, they are happier than ever to be back again with us.

THROWING OUT LABELS

Did you ever get a nickname back in first or second grade that stuck with you for a long time—that you thought you would never get rid of? Did you ever get a reputation for some silly thing that you hoped everybody would forget?

"Fats" Lawson, in fifth grade, was really one of the slimmest boys in the class. He was on the county track team and also played basketball in the neighborhood. But the kids called him Fats, nonetheless.

In fact, only a few remembered why. Only three or four remembered that back in first grade he was the boy with the chipmunk cheeks who used to bring two packages of Twinkies every day in his lunch and gobble them down. He had been slightly overweight back then, and when he stuffed the food in his mouth it make him look even fatter, so everybody called him Fats.

Nobody seemed to notice that in second grade he no longer brought Twinkies. Nobody seemed to notice that in third grade he was no longer chubby. No one even commented in fourth when he went out for track and basketball. And in fifth, when he was actually two pounds underweight for his age and height, nobody even questioned his nickname at all. They just went on calling him "Fats" because they always had.

The problem with labels is that they are sometimes hard to take off. The way a person is in second grade is not necessarily the way he will be in fifth. The way a person eats or dresses or looks in third grade is not the way he will eat or dress or look the rest of his life. Everybody deserves a second chance—or three or four or fifty, even.

Each of us has an off-day once in a while. Or perhaps we are out of sorts for a whole month. We may even have a rough time of it for a year or two. But this does not mean we will be like that forever. Nobody wants to be labeled or remembered for the one period in his life when he was at his worst.

It is important to accept the fact that you and your friends will be changing as long as you live. Just because you are more or less loners right now does not mean you will be loners the rest of your lives. Sometimes a lonely year is followed by a really great one. Nor does this mean that persons who are very popular now can count on that popularity all their lives.

Try not to paste a label either on a friend or on yourself.

"He's dumb"; "she's corny"; "he stinks"; "she's selfish," may describe the way a person is right now, but not necessarily the way he'll be tomorrow.

"I'm stupid"; "I'm inconsiderate"; "I'm un-popular"; "I'm ugly," describes only the way you feel about yourself at a certain point in your life—not necessarily the way you actually are or the way you will be a week or a month or a year from now.

There is always room for improvement, for growth, but don't expect more of yourself than you do of others, or more of others than you do of yourself. Don't sneer at others for grabbing the biggest piece of cake if you would like to grab it first! And if you did grab it first and then began hating yourself because you were so greedy and selfish, remember that a dozen other eyes were on that cake, and every stomach there would have loved it.

Sometimes it's interesting, and rather fun, to look at each of your friends as though you had never seen them before in your life, letting a new impression of them take over instead of the old one.

When you see Lisa coming, for example, try not to let your mind tell you, "Bet the first thing she'll talk about is herself."

Maybe she will, and maybe Lisa hasn't

changed at all. Maybe she's still self-centered and somewhat conceited.

But then again, maybe she is not. Perhaps you're remembering her the way she was in fourth grade, and possibly she's grown a lot since then.

The least you can do is give people a fresh start now and then. If you let your mind be open, you may hear Lisa say when she comes up to you, "That was a very hard test in history yesterday. How did you do?"

If your mind is still set on how self-centered she is, you're probably whispering to yourself, "See? All she can think about is how well she did." But if you hear her with new ears, you may realize that the history test is what everybody has been talking about, and actually, she asked how you were doing.

Make sure that when a friend improves and matures, your opinion can change along with him.

MAKING THE BREAK

Sometimes you may decide that a particular friend or group of friends is not really best for you. Perhaps you became friendly with them when you were lonely or new in school or just because they lived close by or it seemed convenient.

You may have found that these are really not the people you want to be your closest friends. You might even get into trouble if you continue to go around with them and do as they do.

You may wish that you could just open your eyes some morning and find yourself in a strange new place. You wish your father would get transferred and move the family to another state.

But chances are that nothing quite so magical is going to happen. You are going to have to make a break, and you wonder how to go about it.

It is no easier when it's only one friend. Sometimes it's even worse. Some people purposely do something to make the friend angry—promise to come over and then go somewhere else—so that the other person will break off with them. But that's a rather cowardly way of dealing with the problem.

The best, and probably easiest, way is to get

involved in another group or another project so that you will have a true excuse for staying away. Gradually you'll become busier and busier doing other things with other people until your friend or former group realizes that you have lost interest.

Of course it is easier if there's another group or another friend handy, just begging to take you in. What if there's not? What if you know that the friends you have are not good for you, but you don't have any other group in mind—if you don't really feel welcome yet anywhere else?

STARTING OVER

When you finally decide to make a break and start over, prepare yourself for the fact that at times you will be lonely. There will be times when you will feel that even running around with the old gang and getting into trouble is better than sitting home alone with no friends at all.

But not really. You can, for a while, be your own best friend. Use the time alone to work on a hobby or start a project you've always wanted to do.

Learn to ice skate. Read all the books you've never had time to read. See if you can hike to the top of some hill. Explore the east side on your bike. Take guitar lessons. Write a story about what happened to your uncle at the World's Fair.

Becoming involved in a project or hobby not only helps pass the time, but will make you a more interesting person to others as well.

Next, go where you think the kind of people you want to meet would be. If you are interested in plays and dramatics, see if your school has a theater club. Or perhaps you could even start one. If you are interested in volunteer projects and helping others, see what kind of activities your church or synagogue may have. If you like sports, call up the local recreation association and see if they sponsor teams in basketball or soccer or touch football.

Libraries often have book clubs for people your age. Organizations for the blind frequently need others to read books and newspapers to their members. Scout troops plan all kinds of

activities, and YMCA's have courses and classes on things you never even knew about.

No matter what you choose, you will find people there who share your interests. At first you will all be strangers, of course. But as you get to working on a project together or rehearsing a play or printing a newspaper, you will lose your shyness and come to know each other better. Suddenly you will discover that in sharing an experience you have become closer than ever and, without even thinking about it, you're friends.

Don't wait to be invited. If nobody has asked you to a party recently, throw a party yourself. Invite anyone you wish, and don't purposely leave someone off the list just because he didn't invite you to his. If it's someone you want to know better, or think you might like to know, take a chance. Everybody enjoys being invited, even if he can't come for some reason.

Learn to show your honest feelings. If someone invites you out and you want to go, say yes and show that you are happy about being asked. Don't say, "I don't know. I'll tell you later." Playing hard to get is childish.

HELP!

Boys and girls may find themselves in a situation where it seems as though nothing they do is right, and that nobody really likes them. They may feel that they are trying hard to be thoughtful and friendly, but for some reason things just aren't working out.

Perhaps they give a party but only a few children come. Or they may find that even though they join a group which interests them, children, for some reason, seem turned off when they are around. They know there is something about themselves others don't like, but they don't know what it is.

Others may find that even though they want very much to get out of a certain group or a particular friendship, it is not as easy as it seems. Possibly they are even afraid to leave. Perhaps the gang threatens them if they do. Or perhaps a friend seems to need them so much that he or she cries or seems to become actually ill when the relationship is broken.

We can never be everything that someone needs in a friend, no matter how much we try, but some people seem to think that we can and make demands on us that we simply can't meet.

There are professional people who can help us when we have serious problems like these. Teachers can often help us discover what it is about us that others dislike. School counselors know quite a bit about gangs and the way they can control their members. They also know that some people become very dependent on their friends in an unhealthy way. They may be able to work both with you and your friends to make the break easier.

Scout leaders, Sunday school teachers, ministers and rabbis, neighbors and relatives, and certainly parents can all be called upon to help if you are facing a situation with your friends that is difficult for you to handle alone.

Most grownups have been through similar situations themselves or know of such problems. Often they can offer some advice based on their own experiences that would be helpful to you.

Peggy knew that others laughed at her behind her back. She knew that the other girls whispered about her in the lunchroom. She thought about her clothes and her grades, but couldn't see that they were any different from anyone else's. Yet something was different; something made her unwelcome.

She asked to stay after school one afternoon for a heart-to-heart talk with her teacher. Mrs. Epstein was puzzled for a while, too. She seemed to have noticed nothing really different about Peggy in the classroom, but promised to observe her more carefully in the next week and see if she could discover something that would turn the other girls against her. Two days later she had the answer.

In class (she told Peggy) Peggy talked and behaved in a normal manner. But in the lunchroom or on the playground at recess, Peggy spoke in a decidedly childish manner, in a higher-pitched voice than usual. She whined frequently, pouted, and her feelings seemed easily hurt.

"It's as though you suddenly become five years old on the playground." Mrs. Epstein said kindly. "I'm sure you're not even aware you're doing it, but you are."

Peggy thought about it for a long time. And in the lunchroom the next day, when the girls asked her a question and she started to answer, she was aware for the first time that her voice was growing higher and that she was speaking in a little-girl whine.

After a few more chats with her teacher, Peggy and Mrs. Epstein discovered together that since Peggy was the youngest of four children in her family, the others had always treated her as the baby. She had soon learned that growing up in her family the easiest way to get attention or something she wanted was to become childlike, to whine and cry and pout. And this kind of behavior carried over, without her even realizing it, to the playground and the lunchroom.

She made a determined effort to speak normally, to not try to get her way by whining, and gradually she began to notice a change in the other girls. Six weeks later she was invited to a girl's home overnight, the first time that had ever happened.

Starting over may be the best thing you ever did, and also the hardest. It is difficult because no one can really *guarantee* that there is a wonderful, marvelous friend just around the corner if you will only work at changing yourself and your habits. Nobody can write you a contract or promise to like you forever or give you a certificate of popularity.

But if you really try to see yourself as others see you, if you are honest about what you are like and try to find people who share your interests, if you are not afraid of getting help from a counselor or teacher if you are in a situation you can't handle alone, then the chances are very, very, very, very, very good that sooner or later you will discover that you really do fit in, that you really are liked, and—best of all—that you like yourself.

FRIENDS
ARE FOR SHARING

Once you've found some great friends—young or old, silly or serious, popular or loners—what do you do? Keep them a secret? Enjoy them all by yourself? Friends are for sharing, and families usually like to be included.

If, when you walk out the door, your Mom asks, "Where are you going?" and you answer, "Out," she's going to be upset. She can figure that much for herself.

If you say, "Over to Bob Jeffers'," it tells her something, but not much.

If you say, "Over to Bob Jeffers' to play his guitar," that tells her a lot.

And if you add, "Would you like to meet him some time?" that's even better.

If you have the kind of friends you would like to bring home, and the kind of home that welcomes your friends, you're luckier than you know.

Parents can be friends, sisters can be friends, grandparents and uncles and aunts can be friends, and scrubby little brothers with dirt under their nails can be friends. What's more, they can even be friendly with your friends if you'll let them. Every person, every age, has something to contribute.

That's the nicest thing about friendship—you never know when or where it will turn up. Somebody out there likes you—someone you may least expect. And somebody needs you, someone you may not even know.

Don't be afraid to go looking, to make changes, to take chances, because that's what life is all about, and it's certainly half the fun.